Dispatches from the Outer Deep

A Guide to Writing, Editing, Submitting, and Publishing Short and Long Fiction

Matthew Kressel

I0177551

SENSES FIVE

Also by Matthew Kressel

King of Shards
Queen of Static
"The Sounds of Old Earth"
"The Meeker and the All-Seeing Eye"
"The Last Novelist"

And much more at
www.matthewkressel.net

§

This is version A1, and it has an ISBN of 978-0-9796246-4-3.

Published by:
Senses Five Press
Ridgewood, NY, USA
www.sensesfive.com

Cover Art: Tithi Luadthong (Grandfailure)
Cover Design: Kris Dikeman

SENSES FIVE

Contents

Introduction

About Me and Why I Created this Book

WHEN PICKING UP A WRITING ADVICE BOOK LIKE THIS one, the first thing you should ask yourself is this: With all the thousands of other writing advice books out there, what can this book give me that the others cannot?

Let me begin by telling you a little about myself. As of this writing, I've published over seventy short stories in professional fiction markets. I've published two novels and I have two more coming soon. My work has been nominated for three Nebula Awards, a World Fantasy Award, and a Eugie Foster Award. It has appeared in multiple *Year's Best* anthologies. And my short fiction has been translated into ten languages. I'm the co-host of the New York-based Fantastic Fiction at KGB reading series alongside Ellen Datlow. And I published the short fiction and poetry magazine *Sybil's Garage* for seven years. I've been a member of the Altered Fluid writing group for more than two decades. And I'm the creator of the Moksha submissions system, a manuscript submissions manager used by some of the largest fiction publishers today. This is all to say I know a lot about writing!

But when I started my writing career two decades ago, I knew next to nothing. I was greener than a shot of wheat grass.

In 2002, I enrolled in a few classes at the New School in Manhattan (one was taught by the famous editor Alice K. Turner) while working on my writing. Eventually, in 2003, I sold my first short story, "Mortar," to a small market known as *Alien Skin Magazine*.

I was so excited. I thought, *I've made it! I'm a published writer!* I naively assumed that everything would be smooth sailing from then on.

What I found instead was long years of slogging, difficult work, rejection, and frustration. I sold a few stories in those early days, but not as many as I'd hoped. It wasn't until I started editing and publishing *Sybil's Garage*, which I ran from 2003 to 2010, that I finally understood how editors read fiction. A light bulb turned on in my mind, and I suddenly saw why editors stop reading on the first page. I understood how you have to grab and hold a reader's attention *with every single word*. I found that by reading the "slush pile" (the flood of incoming submissions) I became a better writer myself. And with this realization I began to sell more stories.

During this time I became a regular attendee of the Fantastic Fiction at KGB reading series, held at the famous KGB Bar in Manhattan. It was hosted at the time by Gavin Grant and Ellen Datlow. Gavin ran the fantastic Small Beer Press publishing house, and I would regularly pick his brain for advice. In 2008, Gavin he asked me to take over his hosting duties. I had zero experience with public speaking and I'm quite introverted, so I demurred. But, at the prompting of some friends (especially Mercurio D. Rivera) I finally told Gavin yes. And I'm extremely glad I did!

In the past sixteen years – holy smokes, has it been that long? – I've heard about four hundred live readings, including authors William Gibson, Victor LaValle, Lauren Beukes, Joe Hill, Paul Tremblay, Jeffrey Ford, Kelly Link, and *many* others. After hearing so many stories read aloud by so many masterful authors, I've gained a deep intuitive sense of how to engage an audience with words.

Back in 2003, I also joined the Altered Fluid writing group. If you've never heard of Altered Fluid, you might have heard of some of our members: N.K. Jemisin, Sam J. Miller, Alaya Dawn Johnson, and Mercurio D. Rivera, to name a few. The number of awards our members have won or been nominated for is too long to list, but it's impressive. And I've had the immense fortune to have my work critiqued by all of them. I learned much from their critiques, but I also learned an enormous amount by critiquing *their* work. I discovered that seeing flaws in another's work helped me see flaws in my own. I wouldn't be the writer I am without Altered Fluid.

When I first started writing, most manuscript submissions were sent by postal mail. You had to put your printed manuscript in the mail, with a self-addressed stamped envelope, and not only hope your package arrived safely, but that your response made it back safely too. You often had to wait six months, a year, or longer for a reply. But in the mid 2000s, many markets began to go online, and some publishers recognized a need for an online submissions manager. That's why I developed the Moksha submissions system. My first customer was *Lightspeed* magazine. But soon *The Magazine of Fantasy and Science Fiction, Tor.com / Reactor, Uncanny Magazine, Strange Horizons, Apex Magazine,* and many other publishers began to use Moksha. Today, anyone with an internet connection can submit to literally hundreds of publications using Moksha, all for *free*. (We never charge authors.) To date, Moksha has processed over a million submissions from nearly every country on the planet, and that number grows by the thousands each day. Having been an editor myself for many years, I understand editors and what they want. Moksha is designed with them in mind.

I list all these things not to boast, but to point out that, despite my occasionally strong sense of impostor syndrome, I'm highly qualified to talk about the craft of writing, editing, submitting, and publishing short and long fiction. In this book, I share many of the tips, tricks, techniques, knowledge, and more I've gleaned along the way. I hope that it will help you navigate the tricky and often complicated world of fiction publishing.

Some highlights in this book include:

- Why editors stop reading your story on the first page

- Dos and don'ts in the submission process
- Why no two authors' paths will be the same
- Stories and anecdotes about my own creative path
- Pansting vs. plotting, or when to outline
- Why rejections matter
- Why reviews don't
- Emotional health
- & much more

Each chapter of this book originally appeared in my writing advice newsletter, _The Outer Deep_, which I began in 2022, and has been reproduced here with minor edits.

As you read each chapter, all I ask is that you remember that my (or any) writing advice is (a) not absolute and (b) subjective. If these tips work for you, fabulous! I'm happy they do. But I make no claim that these tips will work for everyone, or in all cases. Use what you find helpful. Discard the rest. (Advice useful for life as well as writing.)

Anyway, I hope this book will help you on your own creative path, or at the very least provide you with some joy and entertainment during your day!

Thank you for reading it.

Best,
Matthew Kressel
Ridgewood, NY
March 2024

More at matthewkressel.net

Constructive and Destructive Critiques

I am become Death, Destroyer of Words

IF YOU WRITE FICTION, THERE WILL LIKELY COME A TIME where you'll want to show it to others. This may be to your mother, your friends, or, if you're anything like me, to peers in a writing group.

About twenty years ago I took a writing class at the New School in Manhattan called *Writing Science Fiction & Fantasy,* taught by the late Alice K. Turner. Alice was a fiction editor at *Playboy* for many years (*Playboy* was one of the best-paying markets, if not *the* best, and it was considered a mark of high status to get your work published there.)

There was this young man in the class, let's call him Bob. Bob took on a haughty, holier-than-thou attitude during the class. We would each write a bit of fiction, share it via email, then take turns providing critiques of each other's work.

Bob was never happy with us.

No sentence was innocent. No word beyond reproach. He usually gave long-winded rants laced with pseudo academic-sounding analyses on why this or that element didn't work. He wasn't the teacher, but he thought he was. Bob found most everything distasteful or (heaven forbid) mediocre, and unworthy of his lofty writerly tastes. Except, of course, his own writing.

No one liked Bob very much.

A few years later, I joined the writing group *Altered Fluid* (of which I am still a member today). We had a guest one night, let's call her Zelda. We invited Zelda to our group to critique our stories and dispense professional advice as we were all more or less beginners and Zelda was much further along in her career. Mine happened to be one of the stories being workshopped this evening. During her critique, Zelda told me how much she "loathed" my story, that I knew nothing of my subject, and she was so actively hostile to me and my story that others around the table began to stir uncomfortably in their seats. According to my friends, I took her harsh critique in stride, but I remember feeling mortified.

A few months later my story (mostly unchanged from that evening) went on to be published in a well-regarded fiction magazine. The editor loved it, and to this day I still feel it's one of my most creative and inventive stories.

Flash forward a few years later to when my first novel, *King of Shards*, came out. A reviewer from a small fantasy website panned the book, calling it "clunky", "awkward", and "tedious", the characters "underdeveloped" and "flat", and went so far as to criticize the book cover, the paper type, and font choices (for those who don't know, traditionally published authors have little say in the actual physical book design.) The reviewer seemed *furious* at the very idea that the book even existed.

I was not happy with this review. At all.

But I got more reviews: *King of Shards* was praised by *NPR Books*, the *Barnes & Noble Sci-Fi and Fantasy Blog*, *The Huffington Post*, and *Publisher's Weekly*, to name a few. Even the great N.K. Jemisin loved it and gave me a blurb. Great accolades, for sure. But still that one bad review stung.

The thing is, no matter what you write there's always going to be someone who doesn't like it. You should never hope to please everyone. It's impossible. You should write for one person and one person alone: *yourself*. Write the story you'd love to read.

I promise you that if you love your work, someone else will too. Your passion will come through. Your words will be infused with it.

This doesn't mean you should ignore good advice when it comes. So how do you know if advice is good or bad? When deciding whether or not to use story suggestions I've received, I use the following guidelines:

- If the suggestion is *constructive*, that is, if the critiquer has made an obvious effort to understand the story I'm trying to tell and *their suggestion will improve the story I'm trying to tell*, use it.
- If the suggestion rings true to me, that is, if I feel *the suggestion is in line with what I'm trying to say,* use it.
- These two elements may seem the same, but they are subtly different.
- And, as a corollary, you should never accept bad advice. And how do you know if a suggestion is bad?
- If the advice is *destructive,* that is, if the critiquer has made no clear attempt to understand what I'm trying to say, and they are dismissive, angry, condescending, or disdainful towards me or my work, ignore it.
- If the advice doesn't ring true to me, that is, if I don't feel it will improve the story I'm trying to tell, ignore it.

Also, beware the Destroyer. The Destroyer is usually someone frustrated with their own writing or lack of success, or a writer in a comfortable position of power who can't abide some youngling like yourself nipping at their heels. The Destroyer will project their own frustrations onto you and your work. *How dare you write such a thing!* they will seem to say. *What were you thinking, you fool?*

Avoid Destroyers. They are toxic. And if you can't avoid them, do your best ignore them. Their reactions are not actually about you, but their own disturbed psychology, though that may be hard to see in the moment.

You should also be open to advice from those who aren't writers or editors or have any familiarity with critiquing fiction. Sometimes getting an amateur opinion is better than getting one from a pro. Oftentimes, these "amateur" opinions will be more raw and true, not tempered by the tropes and terminology that writers use. If something isn't working, these "amateurs" will often be the first to spot it. Again, trust your gut. If their suggestion rings true, use it. If it doesn't, don't.

In the creative path there will come along folks who try to destroy your confidence, either intentionally or as a consequence of their behavior. Don't let them.

Cultivating Boredom

Why being bored is actually good for your
imagination

WE LIVE IN INCREDIBLE TIMES. I CARRY AROUND A SMALL
device that, with a few simple taps, I can call up images of
distant black holes, the collected works of Shakespeare, and
the dankest, silliest memes. When I'm waiting on line to check
out at the supermarket, I can check my work email. While
I'm waiting my turn at the dentist's office, I can check what's
trending on social media. While I'm sitting on the toilet, I can
scroll through pretty Instagram pictures. Even watching TV,
if I'm not fully invested in the plot, all I have to do is pick up
my phone and I'm whisked away to another dimension.

This is a technological miracle, and I value having this
ability. But it's a dangerous one. It's a terrible thing to *never* be
bored, to always have one form of media or another piped
into your brain at gigabits per second.

When I was a kid (long ago in the pre-Internet days) and
my friends weren't around, I'd complain to my mother, "Mom,
I'm so *bored*!" And she'd respond in her typical Eastern-
European Jewish curt way, "Then go play with yourself!"

She wasn't trying to be cute or make a gross pun. She
was telling me to *use my imagination*. And one day, amidst
my strongly manifested boredom, I created an adventure in
my backyard to entertain myself. I dreamed up imaginary
characters and galaxy-spanning plots, and I, of course, was
the hero.

I played by myself, but I was never alone.

Something clicked that day, something that's never left
me: I realized that I had the power to control my view of the
world. I realized that *if I used my imagination I would never*

be bored again. This was a revelation to me, and I can trace a direct path from that weekend afternoon many years ago to myself now, a writer, artist, and coder — all tasks that require exercising strong powers of imagination.

SOCIAL MEDIA MURDERS THE IMAGINATION. BOREDOM CULTIVATES IT.

Cal Newport in his excellent book *Deep Work* speaks of setting aside three to four hours every day to turn off all distractions. Silence your phone and disconnect from your email. Remove all potential interruptions. This quiet space allows you to enter what artists call "flow" or "being in the zone," that deeply immersive state of intentional creativity. Getting into a flow state takes practice. It's a muscle that you need to exercise. But with endless, constant interruptions, that muscle atrophies faster than the latest hashtag.

I'd like you to try this experiment: All day today, try to notice how often you reach for your phone when you're bored. Do you reach for it at lunch? While waiting in line for coffee? Between work tasks? How much time do you spend scrolling Twitter / X, Instagram, Facebook, YouTube, or TikTok? Today I'd like you to try something different. Instead of opening that app, put down that phone, and just *sit*.

"And do what?" you say.

Do *nothing*.

Allow yourself to be bored.

Have a look around.

Take in your surroundings.

Have a look at the table. How was it made? Look out the window at the leaves on that tree. Notice their colors. Listen to the sounds of cars or birds or people. Smell the the coffee, pollen, the laundry scent of your own clothing.

Just take in the world. Breathe. Sit.

Without the constant stimulation of social media, you may find things oddly...*quiet.* And uncomfortable.

At this point, you may *really* want pick up that phone. Don't. Examine this feeling some more. Do you feel an almost overwhelming urge to pick up your phone? To check your email? To scan TikTok? That discomfort you feel is a real addiction, your desperate need to get that hit of dopamine from views and likes and subscribes. Social media is deliberately designed this way — to keep you addicted and coming back.

If you feel this pull strongly — and I have felt it too — I'd advise you to read *Ten Arguments for Deleting Your Social Media Accounts Right Now* by Jaron Lanier. Jaron was a pioneer of virtual reality and the early internet, and he was a strong believer in the power of technology to liberate humanity. But he changed his views when he realized how social media was designed to amplify the worst human traits to get advertiser clicks, how it's been engineered to keep you addicted, upset, and most of all *engaged*.

This addiction isn't your fault. You've been hoodwinked by malicious psychologists and morally repugnant technologists hungry for self-profit. They're the equivalent of heroin dealers offering up free samples of their brown powder.

Social media is always free, because they know you'll come back for more.

Social media is the imagination killer. In the realm of free thought that boredom allows, the mind has free space to wander. Instead of drowning your mind with images and videos and ideas that some pernicious algorithm hopes will keep you engaged, boredom means you're stuck with your self alone.

What might you notice on that supermarket check-out line when not scrolling on your phone? What ideas might you dream up on your lunch break if you weren't on Twitter? What new associations and ideas could arise in your mind if you exercise your imagination instead of having your mind exorcised? Boredom allows you the space to be creative. With boredom, you confront yourself and your relationship to others.

Recently I was watching a TV show from the early 2000s with a scene in a coffee shop. I noticed that no one was on their phones. They were reading books or chatting or just sitting and looking out the window. This show was fiction, but it reflects a truth. Before about 2008, before iPhones and Android devices hijacked our attention, before social media infected into our lives, the world looked and felt much different. Now, when I go to my local coffee shop or restaurant, and even the small local bookstore, I see everyone on their phones, even when sitting with others.

I'm not a Luddite. I work in IT. I recognize the ability of technology to liberate humanity. But technology can be a prison too. We've let social media companies pull the wool over our eyes. We've let algorithms and profits suck away our capacity for extended, creative play, which can only happen in a distraction-free space.

The poet and artist William Blake, in his four-fold vision, said that imagination is the greatest human trait, and only by exercising our imagination can we realize our greatest creative potential.

Einstein said, "Imagination is more important than knowledge. For knowledge is limited, whereas imagination embraces the entire world, stimulating progress, giving birth to evolution."

In a recent *New York Times* op-ed, writer David Brooks says, "What happens to a society that lets so much of its imaginative capacity lie fallow? Perhaps you wind up in a society in which people are strangers to one another and themselves."

What happens in a world where we're so constantly distracted, so eager to alleviate even the slightest hint of boredom, that we have no space left over for imaginative play? You get the world we're in now — full of disconnected, paranoid, anxious, and inflexible people. A world where most have trouble envisioning a better world because the current one is continually, constantly, scrolling past us at 240 characters per second.

Set aside time to be bored. You'll not only increase your capacity for imaginative play, you'll see the world differently. You'll allow yourself space to dream up new ideas, to make new connections and associations that you'd never do in a state constant, agitated distraction.

Channeling Your Emotions into Your Fiction

Find that feeling that keeps you up at night and write about it

I WAS ATTENDING A FRIEND'S WEDDING IN SAN FRANSISCO, and while sitting in the hotel with my friend and author, Mercurio D. Rivera, we watched a documentary about the tearing down of the old Yankee Stadium to make way for a new, bigger, "better" stadium on a plot next to the old one. The very idea filled me with rage. While I don't watch much baseball these days, I used to be an obsessive fan and had attended games at Yankee Stadium (the old one) many dozen times. I even snuck into the stadium once, posing as a concession employee, to meet my friends at a sold-out game. I have a lot of memories there.

I thought, *How dare they tear down this place that has so much meaning not only to me, but to so many others! It's the literal "House that Ruth Built," and they're tearing it down!*

I'm also, if you don't know me, a staunch environmentalist. I became one ever since I took a philosophy class in college that made us read *Silent Spring, Pilgrim at Tinker Creek,* Thoreau, and the transcendentalists, among others. To me, the Earth is precious and sacred, even if you (or I) don't necessarily believe in a Deity, capital D.

The rage I felt at them tearing down the original Yankee Stadium, and the rage I felt at the literal tearing down of Earth to make way for condos and strip malls and factory farms and parking lots — all of that went into my story which became known as "The Sounds of Old Earth". In the story, Abner, an older resident of the upstate New York town of New Paltz, is being asked to leave his beloved family home, of which his family has lived in for many generations, to move to New Earth, a brand new planet being constructed beside the old one. The Old Earth, the planet Abner now inhabits, is polluted, corrupted, broken, and its mass is being dismantled, sliced apart like a cake at a birthday, to be used to construct the new planet and to make more and "better" homes for humanity.

Abner doesn't want to go. He loves his old house too much. There are too many memories there. His wife, his kids, his family. Even the frogs, which croak loud on summer evenings, call to mind millennia, even eons, of history, which is all being thrown away...

The Sounds of Old Earth went on to be a finalist for the Nebula Award in 2013. On the day it was published, January 1, 2013, Joyce Carol Oates said, "This is a powerful story that is both tragic & hopeful–unexpectedly. And beautifully written. Thank you for sharing it."

All I did was write what I felt. I channeled my very real, very powerful feelings into a narrative, and the story connected with readers because it connected with me.

Veteran editor Ellen Datlow said, "This is gorgeous, melancholy, and heartbreaking. I highly rec it (I cried through most of it)."

You can't fake emotion. Well, you can. In fact, writers do, and do it often. But the emotions that connect with readers, the stories that make them gasp and start and cry — these come from very real places.

No, I've never lived on a planet that was being dismantled to make another. But I have felt the pain at seeing beloved places being torn apart. And I took that feeling and channeled it into my fiction.

Find that thing that makes you angry, that makes you sad or melancholy or makes you scream with excitement. Find that feeling that keeps you tossing and turning at night, spinning in your mind like an electron around a nucleus, fast

as photons. Find that feeling and write about it.
    If it moves you, others will be moved by it too.

Creating Compelling Characters

How to create fictional characters that keep people reading

WHY DO SOME FICTIONAL CHARACTERS WORK AND OTHER characters feel flat or fake? Why do some characters compel you to keep reading and others make you want to throw the book across the room?

The secret is *depth*, giving your characters more than one personality dimension. Real people are complex, contradictory, emotional bundles of matter and energy, and few people are exactly who they present to be on first blush.

So how do we give our characters multiple dimensions? By recognizing that even good characters — our "hero" protagonists, for example — have dark aspects of their personalities. And, conversely, our "anti-hero" antagonists, the "baddies" in our stories, will often have positive or "good" aspects of their personalities.

A protagonist who is always good, who always does the right thing, who's always happy, bright, and cheery is sometimes called a Pollyanna. After about the age of six, no one likes to read about a Pollyanna. I mean, there probably are folks who do, but if they're out there, I haven't met them. Most adults don't like reading about Pollyannas because they're boring. Pollyannas never surprise us. We always know that, no matter what, the Pollyanna is going to come out at the end of the story smiling and happy. Pollyanna will always do the right thing, happily of course, never deviating from that firm line. That type of security may be comforting for some, but for me it doesn't make very compelling fiction.

And just the same, the antagonist who is always bad, who

is always evil, who is always cruel, bitter, and unforgiving, is often called a Mustache-Twirler (so-called because of the cliche of the evil mastermind twirling his mustache while maniacally laughing). Mustache-Twirlers are boring to read for the same reason: they're predictable. We know how the Mustache-Twirler will react to any situation: with anger and malice (and more mustache-twirling). They are evil because they are evil, so isn't that enough?

No, it's not.

Real human beings have layered personalities, histories, and depth, that go much deeper than superficial details. In *The Undiscovered Self*, psychologist Carl G. Jung speaks of our twin good and evil aspects, two parts of the self that exist in *all human beings*. Many (perhaps most) of us only consciously acknowledge the positive aspect of our egos, our "good" natures. But each of us has an evil side, which we will often bury or suppress, for fear of what it reveals: that we're not always the morally upright, righteous beings we take ourselves to be, and that we can be just as cruel and unforgiving as the worst humans among us.

You see this played out clearly in the U.S. political sphere. Many on the U.S. political Right are convinced that the Left is morally repugnant heathens intent on destroying conservative religious and family values, without recognizing that many of their chosen leaders have little or no such values themselves. Meanwhile, many on the U.S. political Left are guilty of the same cultism, group-think, and hypocrisy they accuse the Right of, without being able or willing to see those dark traits in themselves.

We project our dark sides onto others as a way to absolve ourselves of the self-hate and shame that acknowledging the unwanted aspects of our beings would bring. (For more on this, see *For Your Own Good*, by Alice Miller, which I highly recommend.)

A great example of this playing out in fiction is in *The*

Lord of the Rings. All the heroes in the *Fellowship* claim to be helping Frodo bring the One Ring to Mount Doom for the greater good of Middle Earth. But the Ring brings out the repressed evil side in anyone who bears it (or even comes near it). Galadriel is one of the few of the heroes who consciously acknowledges this.

Galadriel says to Frodo:

"In place of a Dark Lord you would have a Queen! Not dark but beautiful and terrible as the Dawn! Treacherous as the Seas! Stronger than the foundations of the Earth! All shall love me and despair!"

Galadriel, one of the few among the heroes helping Frodo, acknowledges her own evil side. Only Frodo, who is not strong in stature or swordplay, but in *heart and mind*, has the strength to bring the Ring to Mount Doom. And even then, he ultimately fails, and only succeeds in his great mission because of the love of his friend Sam.

The one exception to this metaphor is the dark lord Sauron himself, who's unremittingly evil in the *Lord of the Rings* trilogy, without a corresponding "good" side. But I submit that Sauron (at least during the events of the books) isn't a real character. He never speaks, and he only acts through avatars. Sauron is more of a destructive *force*, like a hurricane. Also, J.R.R. Tolkien made very clear that the *Lord of the Rings* was a metaphor for the encroaching industrial age that was destroying his beloved pastoral England.

Another great example in fiction — if perhaps a bit too literal — is the Force in *Star Wars*. Yoda is very clear when he trains Luke on Dagobah that the Dark Side of the force is always a risk for a Jedi. Its power is seductive, and Luke's rage and fear are easy paths to take him to the Dark Side. When Luke enters the Dark Side Cave and comes upon Darth Vader himself, only to discover that it's his own face under Vader's helmet, the metaphor cannot be more clear. Luke's unacknowledged dark side is his own worst enemy. He must confront his fear and hate or be controlled by it.

Conversely, Darth Vader himself still has a bit of good in him, as we see in *Return of the Jedi*. And we see this played out in the many *Star Wars* sequels when Kylo Ren and Rey struggle to reconcile their two selves — the good and the bad.

While these are all good examples of the twin aspect of our psyches, I feel *Star Wars* generally takes the the metaphor too far. For most characters, the split isn't so perfectly drawn, but a more complex and crooked line that jumps around like a lightning bolt, forking this way and that, depending on circumstance. *Star Wars* oversimplifies a very complex human trait: the dark aspects of our psyche.

In *The Marriage of Heaven and Hell*, William Blake writes:

"Without contraries is no progression. Attraction and repulsion, reason and energy, love and hate, are necessary to human existence. From these contraries spring what the religious call Good & Evil. Good is the passive that obeys Reason. Evil is the active springing from Energy. Good is Heaven. Evil is Hell."

What Blake recognized centuries before Jung explained it in *The Undiscovered Self* is the twin aspect to our human psyche, and that *both are necessary for human existence.*

What does this have to do with creating compelling characters? If you create an all-evil, or all-good character, you're only revealing one part of the human psyche and ignoring the other part. Without the two, you are missing the dynamism, the progressive energy Blake speaks about. Only together, by encompassing both the good and evil aspects of a character's psyche, can you make a character seem real.

You see this played out in fiction in a thousand ways:

- The detective who's great at her job but terrible at being a parent
- The hit man who is a cold-blooded killer but has a

soft spot for acting

- The beloved war hero who continually puts everyone he loves at risk
- The world-class chess player who can't connect socially and has a drug problem
- The astrophysicist who can't accept that science doesn't give all the answers
- The killer robot that likes to watch soap operas

Characters that are all good or all bad are boring. They don't seem real, because they aren't. Real people have multiple aspects to their psyche, conscious aspects that they "believe" themselves to be, their ego, and their unconscious aspects, which they often try to suppress or repress. Together, these parts brings about an energetic dynamism to characters that makes them real.

Next time you write a character, make sure you consider all aspects of their personalities — the part they consciously acknowledge, and the part they sometimes fail to repress. It will make your characters come to life.

Word Count, Shmerd Count

Why your writing speed doesn't matter, but creating good habits does

How fast can you type? 80 words per minute? 120? 500? I recently saw someone on Twitter saying that they could write 1000 words per hour. That's impressive. If that was the only metric that mattered.

Thankfully, it isn't!

I first became obsessed with word counts after reading Stephen King's *On Writing* about twenty years ago, when I read that he writes about 2000 words per day — no matter what. At the time I was logging my daily word counts on a calendar I hung above my desk, which were clocking in at a paltry *few hundred* or so every few days.

I felt guilty. Ashamed. Ineffectual. *I'll never be a writer if I keep this up*, I thought.

The thing is, focusing only on one metric — a daily word count — is not helpful and even destructive to your writing ability. Of course, some people just write really quickly, and more power to them. And certain publishers (ahem, Amazon, ahem) encourage blitzkrieg writing. But I've been writing professionally for about two decades and have published over fifty short stories and two novels in so-called traditional markets. And the one thing I've found that works better than the sole metric of word counts and speed, better than having the right writing desk or your favorite mug or your ideal writing beverage, is this:

You must create a routine.

This is so important that I'll say it another way: without a routine, without a regular practice (and yes, writing is *practice*) you will not progress, you will not get better, and you will never finish anything you started.

A writer waiting for inspiration to strike before sitting down to write is no different from an aspiring professional musician waiting for inspiration to strike before she practices. A writer waiting for the "right" time to sit down to to write will never find *any* time to write. Decades will go by and you'll say, "If only I'd written that thing…" I've seen it happen, and it makes me sad.

Sure, some days inspiration will flow like rivers. But most days you'll be at the keyboard *just doing the work.* And it's those days where that voice in the back of your head will be telling you: *you must write a million words today! As fast as humanly possible! Faster, even! Get that vomit draft out, you lazy fool! Why aren't you working harder?* But then you slog along, only writing a few hundred words before you tire. You might be tempted to judge yourself for not doing enough.

Resist that temptation. Be patient with yourself. Creativity is a sly beast. Like a muscle, it tires, and ego (both the good and bad aspects of it) is the great creativity killer. If you do the work regularly (for me, it's about twenty hours per week) you'll make progress. Put ass in chair, and I promise you that you'll soon see results.

You may think that since you only wrote a few hundred words, or only for an hour today, or because you didn't finish that first draft that you're somehow failing. But writing happens when we're away from the page too. We might be in the shower, or going for a walk, or out with friends (for me, it's on the treadmill at the gym) when an idea comes — a great scene or story event or poignant character choice. You have to be open and ready for these moments. Carry a paper and pen with you. Or if you're like me, dictate the idea into your phone's note app. (It's fun and frustrating to see my phone try to interpret made-up proper names.) You have to understand that writing is a way of looking at the world, of seeing that your *life experience* is feeding your writing brain too, and that the number of words you wrote today is far less important than the quality of the experience you have conveyed through words.

Some people call this quality vs. quantity. Or writing vs. typing. I tend to resist dichotomies. The world isn't so simple. Instead, I focus on a feeling. Do I feel as if I've put in the work today, that I made an effort? If so, that's enough.

Yes, there are days when it's a struggle to sit down and write. And on those days I force myself to just do the work. As much work as I can. Often, and to my surprise, a few days later when I go back and reread what I've written I find those words actually aren't so bad. In fact, I'm often surprised at how, later, *I'm unable to tell which words I wrote on my "slog" days and which words I wrote on my prolific days.*

Inspiration is great, yes, but doing the work, day after day after day, can lead to great things too.

Make writing a habit and word counts won't matter.

The Dreaded First Page

How you can keep editors reading your story
past the first page

IF YOU DON'T KNOW, ABOUT ELEVEN YEARS AGO I CREATED the Moksha submissions system, a manuscript content manager for publishers. (If you're interested, here's a brief history about it: https://moksha.io/history/). In 2021, Moksha processed about 100,000 submissions from all over the globe. In 2022, it's set to break that record. The top five science fiction and fantasy magazines using Moksha can, during peak periods, easily receive over 100 submissions *per day*.

Now, imagine that you're an editor at one of these magazines. Say you're an average reader, which means you read about 250 words per minute. And now imagine you accept stories where the average length is around 5,000 words. That means the busiest magazines, during peak times, receive about 500,000 words per day. That's five, full-length novels per day, or about 33 hours of reading, per day!

Impossible for one person, of course. Unless you've got a TARDIS. And maybe not even then.

This is why magazines hire *slush readers* (also known as *first readers*). Slush readers are so-called because the manuscripts, back in the snail-mail paper days, used to come in by the bucket load over the transom and pile up behind the editor's door like puddles of slush. Of course these busy magazines have a small army of slush readers, and so maybe each person is reading a dozen stories per day. Still, at 5,000 words a pop, that's 60,000 words per day. Combine this with the fact that most slush readers have day jobs, other responsibilities, families and loved ones to spend time with, food to eat, things they might want to read and watch for pleasure, and, you know, a need for sleep. So here's the ugly little secret that isn't such a secret at all:

Slush readers usually won't finish reading your story unless they absolutely love it. In fact, plenty of times slush readers won't even finish your first page.

When I first started writing, these facts were abhorrent to me. I thought: *How dare they not finish reading the work I spent so many hours laboring on! Don't I at least deserve a thorough read and review?*

In an ideal world, yes. But in reality, there just isn't time.

Years ago I started a small fiction and poetry magazine called *Sybil's Garage*. And when my brain switched from writing mode to editor mode, when I began reading a few dozen submissions a day, I saw the world through a new lens, and my mind was blown. I saw what editors see: that it's often apparent on the first page, typically within the first paragraph, whether or not you're going to enjoy reading a story.

Now, of course, I don't speak for *all* slush readers or editors. I know several editors at popular magazines who make heroic attempts to read *every* word submitted to them. Bless their diligent (and insane!) hearts. But they're a minority. Most slush readers can tell on the first page whether or not your work is going to be good. And since they have dozens of other submissions to read, why waste time reading something they're not going to accept anyway? They've got a dozen more works to read before dinner, and they're tired.

So, how do you make sure to keep editors reading your work? How do you rise above the easily rejectable slush? Here are several things that, when I was an editor, made me put down a submission and stop reading:

MAKING SPELLING, GRAMMATICAL, OR FORMATTING ERRORS ON THE FIRST PAGE

Nothing is a faster turn off than showing on the first page that you don't have a strong grasp of spelling or grammar, especially when all modern word processing software, even free ones, have spelling and grammar checks built in. A big one is mistaking "their" and "they're", "its" and "it's", etc. I've made exceptions for authors for whom English wasn't their first language and older folks who weren't as tech savvy with word processing software. But in general you should never expect an editor to be forgiving. Ruthlessness is their game — it has to be — so make sure your manuscript has perfect spelling and grammar throughout. (An exception, of course, is if you're writing in a specific dialect or style that intentionally goes against so-called Standard Written English; but editors are smart, and they can tell what's intentional and what's just an author being sloppy.)

NOT FOLLOWING SUBMISSION GUIDELINES

This is a big one. You ask for fantasy stories that are less than 3,000 words. An author sends you an 15,000 word horror story. You ask for manuscripts in a Times New Roman font and Standard Manuscript Formatting. The author sends you a manuscript in Comic Sans, with 100 MB of embedded maps. (I once received a glossy author headshot and a several page resume in the mail, none of which was asked for in the guidelines). If you can't be bothered to read and follow submission guidelines, why should an editor bother to read and respond to your work?

I can't say this enough: *respect an editor's time!*

NOT STARTING THE STORY WHERE THE STORY STARTS

Your protagonist sits in a bar, having a beer, pondering the bittersweet symphony of life. They look at the dark clouds and notice how rainy it's been. Your narrator begins a 3,000-word discourse on the history of your world's kingdoms. Your protagonist goes to the store to buy some milk and bread, which has no bearing at all on the story.

You must start the story where the story starts.

Start your story the exact moment where something changes, where something interesting happens, where some impetus arrives that gets your story moving. This doesn't have to be a glorious battle or violent clash of armor and lasers. It could be something as simple as your character receiving a text, hearing a sound, noticing that the knife on the counter is not where she left it last night. But a common problem I see in beginning and veteran writers alike is starting the story too soon. Stretching your writing muscles is fine. Warming up is okay. You may need to know your world's entire history of magical technocracy, whether it rained last Tuesday, or how your protagonist just went to the store right before you start your story-proper, but if that's not where the story begins, cut it. Be ruthless.

THE "WHITE ROOM" SYNDROME

White-room syndrome is the name for a problem common with beginning writers: not establishing a clear sense of place. You have one or more characters speaking to each other...*somewhere.* Inside a house? A factory? A spaceship?

No, no, they're outside!

Great! In a city park? A dense forest? A school playground? You don't have to describe your setting in infinite detail, down to the type of wainscoting, but you need to give the reader *enough* detail for her to create an image of the scene in her mind. Usually, I find one or two salient details is enough. Perhaps you describe the smell of an old house. The metallic grind of machines in a factory. The subliminal throb of a spaceship's engines. If your characters are outside, you might describe the sound of children playing, or the call of a mourning dove in the trees, or the way that old man, sitting all alone on a park bench, makes the protagonist feel melancholy. Let us know *something* about the present location, so the reader can form what John Gardner calls the "fictive dream," or vision of the narrative in your imagination. Without this, the reader will have trouble envisioning your tale.

THE CIPHER PROTAGONIST

Another problem I see a lot in fiction is not knowing who the protagonist is or what she wants. Of course, there are plenty of narratives where having a mysterious protagonist doing mysterious things can work. Lots of Gene Wolfe's work comes to mind. But generally you want to let your reader know what your protagonist wants, and why it's important to her, as soon as possible. Sure, you can have your protagonist enter a smoky bar to hand over a mysterious package, leaving us guessing what's going on — but we still sense there's *meaning* in this transaction, even if that meaning is hidden from us. Why is knowing what your characters want a good thing? Because then the reader can *want alongside them*. Reading is, at heart, an empathetic act. We feel along with the characters, we are along for the ride with their joys and their sufferings. If we don't know what your characters want, what they feel, and why they're upset when their desires are frustrated, then we can't connect with them. You absolutely want your readers to connect with your characters, as this is the number one way to keep them turning pages. Note that this doesn't mean they have to *like* your characters, only that they understand their motivations. We have to know enough about your characters *to experience your story alongside them*.

OVER-DESCRIBING

The opposite of the "white room" syndrome and the "cipher" protagonist is over-describing. You have a fantastic vision of a far-future city that you desperately wish to get onto the page. So you describe, in excruciating detail, the metallurgy, architecture, culture, fashion, and transportation systems using seventeen adjectives, fourteen adverbs, and fifty one made up proper nouns in the first paragraph alone. I did this a lot when I first started writing. I felt I had to get every last detail from my head onto the page. Otherwise, how could the reader see what I was trying to convey? The thing is, the reader will make up her own vision of your story whether you like it or not. She will use her own experiences to conjure up the reality you're trying to convey, and no amount of verbiage is going to transmit that exact image and sensation into her mind. I love dense, flowery, descriptive writing as much as anyone, but in general, unless you are going for a specific style, I find it's usually best to *suggest,* rather than inundate. A few really sharp, really vivid details is enough to conjure an image in the reader's mind. In other words, *let the reader do most of the work for you.*

Inundating the reader

A second cousin of over-describing is inundation. You've kept your adjectives and adverbs in check, good for you. But in the first paragraph you introduce six characters, two with similar-sounding names, one who's first called "Kimberly" and then later called "Kim", then you mention nine different cities, and eight fiefdoms. This firehose of information has the risk of confusing your readers. Sure, they *could* slow down, go back and re-read your sentences and parse everything out. But this is a big ask of editors who have 60,000 words to read between finishing their day job at 5pm and eating dinner with their family at 6pm. You should be striving for reader *immersion*, and too much information at once risks breaking that.

In computer science, there's an old adage known as "seven plus or minus two." It means that most people can only hold 5 to 9 items in their short term memory at once. Beyond this threshold, they get confused. This logic was used in early User Interface, or UI design. I think a similar logic applies in story-telling. Don't inundate the reader with information too quickly. Learning this balance is hard, since *you* know your story well, but your readers won't. You have to imagine what it's like to encounter your world for the first time.

Making readers work a little can be good. Readers love figuring things out on their own, and they will love you for it. But if you make them work too hard, you risk breaking their immersion. And you want editors to keep reading your story, to feel and see and experience along with your characters.

If you ever get the chance, I highly recommended reading slush for a while. It will change your perspective on how others read your stories.

Pantsing vs. Plotting

In the matchup between outlining your story and writing by the seat of your pants, which method comes out victorious?

IF YOU HANG AROUND WRITERS ENOUGH (YOU SHOULD; we're an eccentric bunch) you'll hear them speak about two types of writers: the Pantser (also known as the Gardener) and the Plotter (also known as the Architect).

The Pantser is so-called because she "flies by the seat of her pants." She figures things out as she goes along. She might have a general idea where the story's going, but she lets her instincts guide her path. And she's okay with surprises.

The Plotter, on the other hand, does just that: she plots. She outlines. She has rigid guidelines which she wants to follow, and she hews to it like a tight-rope walker crossing a rocky chasm.

I've used both methods in my work, and I will outline some of the benefits and drawbacks of each here.

THE BENEFITS OF PANTSING

Writing by the seat of your pants is fun. You start with a basic premise, for example, a far-future universe where humanity has long since gone extinct. In my Nebula-nominated short story, "The Meeker and the All-Seeing Eye," I did just that. Right before I went to bed one night, the opening line came to me, almost out of thin air:

"As the Meeker and the All-Seeing Eye wandered the galaxy harvesting dead stars, they liked to talk."

I liked this immediately and wrote it down on a little yellow sticky note (one of these days I have to see if I can find it). It was evocative — who was the Meeker and this All-Seeing Eye? And harvesting dead stars, what was that all about?

I took that line and ran with it, fleshing out the characters. Well, the Meeker should be meek, shouldn't he? And the All-Seeing Eye, well she needs to be all powerful, of course. And what's this part about harvesting dead stars? Ah, yes, they're *billions* of years in our future, and many stars have burnt out. And why do they harvest dead stars? Maybe because the All-Seeing Eye needs the mass for her enormous computer mind. *Yes!*

The story opened up much like this. I honestly had no idea where the story was going as I began. But as I progressed, the world began to unfold. Soon, they uncover an artifact, which encodes an ancient human woman named Beth. Why is this woman there? Someone left a record of her in space? Why? As a *weapon*, of course, against the malicious All-Seeing Eye. But how could one destroy an all-powerful being? By exploiting its one weakness: the Eye's insatiable curiosity.

Pantsing affords you an enormous amount of creativity. At any moment, *anything* can happen, and the writer often doesn't know how things will play out. This is how things develop in real life too. Sure, you have a daily schedule, and you mostly stick to it. But unexpected things will happen. Your plans are foiled by life. Sometimes these changes are mundane, like if someone reschedules a meeting. But sometimes they are life-changing, like when you find out a loved one has unexpectedly died.

One of the things I've discovered is that if the writer doesn't know where the story is going, then the reader likely doesn't either. Sometimes knowing where the story is heading can be exciting: we sense there's a great battle on the horizon, and the build up to that is thrilling. But when the story takes an unexpected turn slantways or leftways, it creates a sense that the world you created is dynamic and shifting, and this can give a sense of verisimilitude and possibility that your story might otherwise lack.

We've all read those books where, by the end of Act I, we can predict where the story ends. And while those kinds of stories can still be fun, there are often few surprises, and you can risk boring your reader: *Ah, yes, I know where she's going. Sigh. I wonder what's on TikTok...*

Another interesting thing that happens when you're writing in pantsing mode, is that you might find your characters take on minds of their own. Sure, you thought you'd have your protagonist go off to fight the evil baddie, but she desperately wants to go to the underground club and dance until the wee hours. And when this happens, that's an excellent sign that you've created a strong character. The *worst* thing you can do, when this happens, is to shoehorn your character into your preconceived plot when she's telling you that she'd much rather do something else. Your readers will say to themselves, *I don't believe Kim Protagonist would ever do that,* and you risk frustrating them. If your characters tell you what they want to do, *my god, listen to them!*

But one of the risks of pantsing is that you find yourself three quarters of the way through your story and *you're nowhere near the end.* Real life doesn't have neat little chapters and acts. It's messy and convoluted. But books and stories need to end. In the pantsing mode, you might find yourself deep in the woods with no idea how you got there, and you're not sure which direction to turn. This is when you end up with a first draft of 500,000 words. Maybe if you're Brandon Sanderson, that's fine. But for most of us, we need to come to a satisfactory conclusion much sooner.

So I suggest this for the pantser: it's okay to wander, but make sure you look up and get your bearings from time to time, so you don't end up too far out in the weeds.

THE BENEFITS OF PLOTTING

Plotting, on the other hand, has one great benefit over pantsing: knowing the ending in advance, you can coordinate all your plot threads to converge on a powerful emotional payoff. In my story "The Sounds of Old Earth" (also a Nebula Finalist), I plotted out the story from beginning to end before I began. I wrote a sentence or two for each scene and filled in the details later.

Abner is an old man who is being forced to relocate to New Earth, a brand new planet created to replace the diseased and dying old Earth. But Abner's home holds so much history. It's been in his family for generations. He's gone to sleep each summer night to the sound of croaking frogs. He can't dream of giving up his ancestral home.

I knew how I wanted the story to end. I won't spoil it if you haven't read it, but let's just say I wanted the ending to be poignant. But I had to get the reader engaged with Abner's plight. I interspersed scenes of Abner walking around his dying town (dying both literally and figuratively) juxtaposed with flashbacks of his former joy. The contrast was striking, and I found myself tearing up. I wasn't the only one. Ellen Datlow said of the story, "This is gorgeous, melancholy, and heartbreaking. I highly rec it (I cried through most of it)."

I don't think my story would have had the same emotional effect if I had "pantsed" it. That's not to say that you can't have an emotional effect by pantsing. Jeffrey Ford says he starts with a premise and just goes with it. He never outlines, and I find his stories are often powerfully affecting. But in my case, outlining the story before I wrote it allowed me to perfectly juxtapose the high and lows to take the reader on a (hopefully pleasing) emotional rollercoaster, which lands exactly where I want them to.

The benefit of outlining is this: foreknowledge. Your puzzle pieces can fit together perfectly, and when done well the payoff can be immensely satisfying.

There are some drawbacks when outlining, though, which is why I don't always use the technique. For one, stories that hew to an outline too perfectly can sometimes seem wooden and rigid. Characters may do unlikely things in order to fit the plot, which risks alienating your readers. Also sometimes, when writing from an outline, you may find that, when things are fleshed out, the outline is too simplistic. You may need to change a plot point to make things more believable. Or you may find that one thing that sounded great in an outline doesn't actually work when you fill in all the details. When his happens, it's always better in my opinion to change the outline to fit the story rather than the opposite. The story must always come first.

The last thing I'll say about outlining is: beware the quicksand. I've seen some writers get so stuck in outlines and research and plotting, that they have collected dozens of pages of outlines and notes for their novels and stories, but have never actually written any words of prose. Outlining should be a tool to help you write your story. It should not become a substitute for one.

So which is better, the Pantser or the Plotter?

The answer is: whichever one works better for you. If you like to plan things out in detail before you begin something, if you want to know every small detail in advance, and if you like to have a guide map to lead you along, plotting might work better for you. But if you are the wandering type, the explorer, who is okay with getting lost, who just follows where the trail leads you, then pantsing might work better for you.

If you are new to writing, I suggest outlining at first, because it will teach you about story structure and plot beats. But be prepared to abandon this technique later when you have a better sense of how to craft a story. (Some never stop plotting, which is okay too.)

For me, I began my writing life as a pantser, then switched

to being a plotter, and now I use an amalgam of the two. I usually have a general idea where I want my story to go, but I let the characters guide me (for me, character must always come first). And sometimes, depending on the project, I choose one method over another.

Recently, for example, I was hired to write a story for a new tie-in media project, and they asked me for an outline before I submitted a story. And while my first draft adheres to my outline closely, I've found that I need to significantly shift certain things, because as I fleshed out the story, some of the protagonist's characterization needs further development not included in my original outline.

So, what are you? A pantser? A plotter? Something else? Do you like having an outline to follow, or do you just go where the story leads? I'll end with this important point: Every person is different and there's no "correct" way to write a story. Anyone who says otherwise is just trying to sell you something.

Should I write every day?

You may not be able to write every day, but you should try to

WHEN I FIRST STARTED WRITING BACK IN 2002, I'D proudly scrawl my daily word count on a nature calendar I hung over my writing desk. Inside the little rectangular boxes, I had penned in 3,851 and 9,234 and 5,199 and 8,654. And you might be thinking, *Wow, he sure was prolific.* Except there was one problem: I might write 8,000+ words one day, and then I'd not write anything for *days, or even weeks.*

If you've read my earlier chapter, "Word Count, Shmerd Count", I explained why word counts don't matter. You're not in a race, trying to beat some arbitrary high score from your fellow writers. Sure, some writers are more prolific than others, but numbers aren't a good metric to decide if you've been productive.

Back in those early days, I'd wait for *inspiration.* I'd wait until I had an idea fully formed in my head or some soul-shaking impetus fueled by caffeine and — *ahem* — other substances. But here's the thing: inspiration is overrated. Sure, it's great when it comes: that idea that comes to you like a divine gift or lightning strike, that so seizes you with energy that it's all you can think about. But such moments are rare. Waiting for them is like sitting around waiting for life to come to you, rather than going outside and bringing yourself to life.

We're all busy. We have spouses or jobs or kids or illnesses to manage or chores to do or that TV show that everyone at work is talking about to finish watching before sleep. But if you want to be a writer, you don't need a special desk, or favorite coffee mug, comfy slippers, brown-label Nag Champa (yes, I used to burn incense when I write), or an inspiration-scented candle. The only thing you need to do is *write*. You have to make writing a part of your life the way brushing your teeth is (I hope brushing your teeth is a part of your life).

You have to make writing routine.

Find a schedule that works for you. Maybe it's late at night, after everyone has gone to sleep. Maybe it's on your lunch break (I know someone who wrote a novel on his one-hour lunch breaks, god bless him). Maybe it's in the morning, before work. I'm an independent contractor — my own boss — so I write weekday mornings before work. I try to get at least two hours of solid writing in. But if the words are flowing, sometimes I go as long as four hours. (I find, however, that after about four hours I need to take a break.)

Mute your phone and shove it under a couch pillow, so you won't check it, and notifications won't distract you. Stay off social media. If you don't need the internet (and trust me, you don't need the internet; that research can wait) consider turning off your wifi. Shut out the world. This is your time. Ten words or ten thousand, it doesn't matter. This is your moment for deep work, the kind of focused, sustained concentration that's necessary for any creative art. I promise you, the outside world will still be there when you return.

So now you're writing. Great! Eventually, you're going to reach a tall hill at some point in your work and need a pause. You're going to want to check social media. You're going to want to get a snack from the fridge. And, hey, have you noticed how dirty the kitchen counter is? And that toaster sure needs its crumbs emptied, and, and, and…

Next thing you know, you've got all the cleaning solutions out and you're scrubbing the tub. Congratulations, you're procrastinating! Resist the urge to step away from the keyboard. Sure, go to the bathroom. Stretch (for god's sake, take care of your back!). But do not heed the siren call that wants you to do anything but write. You won't smash your ship on the rocks, but you won't get any writing done that day, or ever.

And I promise you this: if you make a schedule out of writing, if you write everyday (or *most* days) your brain will remember. It's the same kind of memory that happens when you go to type "happens" and your fingers type "matter" (Just ~~matter~~ happened to me now). It's the same kind of memory that allows basketball players to sink a basket without thinking about it, and it's the same kind of memory that lets guitarists jam a solo without glancing at the fretboard. Our brains are plastic. Not actual plastic (though that might make a cool story). We're malleable. We can learn. If you teach your brain that at a certain time of day, when you're sitting before your keyboard, this is when you create, your brain will say, *Oh, I'd better switch on the creative juices!*

I've experienced this many times. After those slogging early days, I eventually disciplined myself into a better writing schedule where I was writing (almost) every morning. Some mornings, instead of writing, I had to go visit a client in Manhattan. Sitting on the crowded subway, speeding under New York's labyrinthine streets, my brain would unexpectedly bloom with a thousand story ideas. These ideas came from seemingly nowhere, because I wasn't consciously thinking of my story. So what was happening? The reality soon became clear: Normally at this time I'd be writing. And my brain, used to the regular schedule, was like, *Okay, pal, let's do this. Let's create!* I had trained my brain to do creative work at a certain hour, and my brain, that dutiful servant showed up, eager and ready.

And now here's the best part: that burst of creative ideas is no different from so-called "inspiration." The feeling (to me, at least) is identical. But now, instead of waiting for inspiration to strike, you show up each day, playing inside your imagination, and *you bring inspiration to you*. It's a proactive thing. It's like physical exercise. It's work, though it's not that hard (though it may seem so at first). It's just a matter of putting in the sustained effort.

Like lifting weights, it may feel a slog at first. You may only churn out 100 mediocre words. Your story won't be working. You feel you lack "inspiration." You stare at an empty page. But something will happen, eventually, if you keep this up, day after day, if you engage in imaginative play and dedicate the kind of deep focus needed for sustained creative work: it will get easier. At some point, you'll be inundated with so many ideas, you won't know where to put them. (Write them down, somewhere. Maybe they're not right for the current story, but they might work for something else.)

Create a schedule and stick to it. It may be difficult at first to avoid distractions and your desire to do something else. And it may take a while to see results, but eventually the magic will happen: inspiration won't find you, *you'll find it*.

Oh, and one last thing. In regard to needing the perfect writing space in order to write, I wrote *King of Shards* and *Queen of Static* and a few dozen short stories on an ergonomically challenged snack tray that did hell to my back. (Kids, do not try this at home).

Location doesn't matter. But schedules do. Show up, and your inspiration will show up too.

Social Media and Writers, a Match Made in Purgatory

Is social media necessary for writers?

I'm old enough to remember a time before the internet, before cell phones, when after school I'd come home to an empty house, nuke myself a turkey dog in the microwave, then bike over to a friend's house for the afternoon to skateboard or play video games on his Commodore 64. I had to be home before dinner, but other than that, my parents had no idea where the hell I was.

Nowadays, I have family members who share their locations with each other via an app. When I asked my sister about my nephew's whereabouts, she simply checked her phone and said (to my shock), "Oh, he's just at his girlfriend's house." (I skillfully avoided letting my parents know I had a significant other, a feat near-impossible today.)

My sister was similarly able to, using the same app, time the impending arrival of my brother-in-law to the minute. Never mind the Big Brother overtones of this surveillance, the days of just wandering, disconnected and free, are gone.

In 2003, when I started *Sybil's Garage* magazine with a bunch of writer friends, I asked if Cory Doctorow could mention it on his blog, *Boing Boing*, which at the time was one of the most popular SF/F blogs. Cory replied with (I'm paraphrasing), "You need to have more than just a boring web page. You need something people can interact with, like a blog, and other interesting things." That's when I first started writing blog posts[1]. Around the same time, a site called *LiveJournal* became popular. It was a blog too, but you

---

1   You can find an archive of them here: https://www.sensesfive.com/news/

didn't need to have your own website. Anyone could sign up. And it was free. I crossposted most of my blog posts from my website at sensesfive.com to *LiveJournal*, or as the hip kids called it, *LJ*.

The '00s were an exciting time. Small presses sprung up like flowers as the cost of publishing software and production plummeted. Zines like *Sybil's Garage*, and *Electric Velocipede*, and *Say*, and *Lady Churchill's Rosebud Wristlet* where where new writers cut their teeth. Blogs became long-form discussions between authors and readers, and the comment sections, on a hot post, was something that got everyone discussing on and offline for weeks. The word *kerfuffle* grew in popularity.

Then something changed around 2008. Everyone moved to Facebook. I remember being ambivalent about it at first. I already had a *LiveJournal* and a blog, but everyone seemed to be on the Face, so I relented and joined.

It didn't take long before I noticed a disturbing trend. People posted to LiveJournal less often. Blogs slowed and died. Instead, everyone posted to Facebook. This was okay, in theory. People only needed to visit one site to see what their writer friends were up to, not twenty or fifty. If I followed all the same people on Facebook, I should get all the same information, right?

Well...

What I didn't anticipate is that Facebook was now the arbiter of whose posts I saw, and so one day I said to myself, *Self, you know, I haven't heard from Jane Writer in a while*. Turns out, Jane Writer was still posting on Facebook as regularly as she had posted on LiveJournal and her blog, but some hidden algorithm at Facebook decided her posts weren't worth seeing. So I began to wonder what else was being hidden from me.

A couple years later, in 2010, I joined Twitter (now known as X). I resisted it for a long time. Facebook at least had the ability to write long-form posts. Twitter was limited to 120 characters (now 240). Twitter reminded me of those scrolling tickers, or chyrons, you see on the bottom of news programs, short excerpts that were ledes for a larger story. Except, most of the time, there was no "larger story" on Twitter.

Marshall McLuhan said "The medium is the message," and on Twitter that proved to be very true. People were trained to tailor their messages to the limited form, searching for pithy, gut-punching statements that got you to engage, because engagement means more likes and more retweets and even more engagement. Scrolling on Twitter felt to me like sitting at the pointy end of a streaming firehose and trying to take just a sip of water. I hated it from the start.

As I write this, Twitter is undergoing a Phoenix phase as X. (Let's see if she'll be reborn, or go down in flames.) And Facebook seems to have been relegated to greying Gen X'ers and not-retiring-anytime-soon Boomers. Instagram is still popular, and there's also Reddit, which I browse from time to time, and the elephant in the room: TikTok.

Recently, I heard that teenagers and folks in their 20s use TikTok as their primary source of information. "How do I do laundry?" Ask TikTok. "How does the U.S. Government work?" Ask TikTok. *You mean they don't Google it anymore?* I remarked to my wife, horrified. (She shrugged.) Meanwhile, my wife's father once apparently said, when she asked for a computer for school, "What do you need a computer for? We have an encyclopedia in the basement!"

The point is, times change, and with them our means of communication. Once we used cuneiform tablets and didn't use the number zero (we thought it was the devil's number). Now, I can sit at this complex metal and plastic device, punch little raised symbols on a board, and instantly someone can grok my meaning halfway across the world, even if we don't speak the same language. Any sufficiently advanced technology, Arthur C. Clarke said, is indistinguishable from magic. And if computers aren't magic, what is?

I have no doubt that in twenty years, X, Facebook, TikTok, Instagram, Twitch, Mastodon, BlueSky, Threads and all the myriad other social media sites will be obsoleted with something new, and all these young people using their new iMind device will look at all the now forty-something TikTok users who still use physical phones and not brain implants and think-speak to their friend, *QuarkGirl2050*, "How quaint. She still TikToks."

As writers, most of us desire others to be able to read our work. And like Cory Doctorow told me almost two decades ago, with all the glut of information fire-hosing at people every day, *unless you remind people about the work that you do*, they won't notice you, and likely they will forget or move on.

Social media, then, might be a good way to remind them, But social media is also a sharp double-edged sword:

It's a tremendous time-suck. Time spent scrolling social media is time away from writing. I've been in the room with several writers with huge (50K+) Twitter followers, and all they seem to do is check their phones. None of them seemed happy while doing it. It was more like an addiction.

Social media is also controlled by opaque entities and algorithms. Hidden manipulators are controlling what you see[2]. Twitter didn't sell for $44 Billion just because it has silly memes. Imagine being able to control what a billion people hear and see. That's why it's so valuable.

Social media also rewards negative human emotions like anger, frustration, and dread. Rage engages. There's a reason why the temperature on Twitter's always boiling.

But I also believe that social media is, quite unfortunately, the best medium we have at present to let people know about

2   I know that federated sites like Mastodon have fewer filters, so you are basically seeing everything that you want, but this is a minority of social media sites.

our work. Until something better comes along, I think we're stuck with it.

So I use social media in the following ways: I limit my time on social media to less than thirty minutes a day. I try to only post items relevant to my creative life, like a recent 3d artwork I made, or a review of one of my forthcoming short stories, or my novel progress. I don't use it to learn about "trending"[3] topics or world news, and I avoid engaging in subjects that I know will get me riled up, because I know the medium is *hoping* I'll have that reaction, so I will engage more. Engagement is profit for them and toxic for me.

(By the way, I highly recommend the books *Deep Work* by Cal Newport, and *Ten Arguments for Deleting Your Social Media Accounts Right Now* by Jaron Lanier, if you are struggling with social media addiction.)

This is also part of the reason why I started a newsletter. It allows me to connect more closely to those with similar interests on a medium not filtered by a sketchy third party. Anyone who subscribes can read my posts. Each recipient is their own filter, not some hidden malicious algorithm or shady corporate interests.

So — do writers need social media? Alas, I think they do.

It's an unfortunate circumstance of our present reality. But we need to see social media as a tool and not an end in itself. It needs to serve us, rather than us serving it. We should take control of our social media use and only use it in ways that benefit us, and avoiding or dropping it when such use becomes toxic.

This way, when the medium changes, as it most certainly will, we will be more ready to adapt to whatever comes next.

---

3   Who decides what news is "trending"? I'm very suspicious of what others want me to pay attention to, especially when money and power is involved.

Some Thoughts on AI-Generated Content

Things are gonna get real weird soon...

As I write this, there's a big protest going on at Artstation against AI generated images. Personally, I think we, as a society, aren't ready for what AI-generated media will bring. As a writer, I'm terrified that someone soon will be able to say "write me a sci-fi novel about black holes" and the AI will spit out a 120,000-word book that some publisher might actually print and the average reader might consider "good." I labor over each word, sentence, chapter, and overarching story, and most novels take me over a year to write. And now someone will soon recreate this with a few mouse clicks. Terrifying.

This is also happening in the digital art world. Digital artists are rightfully terrified that this tech is coming for their jobs. And another thing to consider is that AI-generated media uses *existing* media as its source material. It's only generating a sort of average of all the media it's consumed. So in a way, AI art (and other media) is profiting off of (many) others' labor.

Now you might say that all artists do this in a way — we absorb media from everywhere and use that to color our own work. But in this case the AI is *literally* using that media to generate new media, like a meat grinder. I foresee a day not too long from now when AI art will use as its source material more AI art, and that's when things will start to get really weird.

What happens when the AI influences itself? Do we get an infinite pattern, like pointing a camera at itself, like putting two mirrors together? I don't think we'll get sentience. More like a flattening of novelty in the arts, and a tendency towards some dull mean.

For the record, I don't think we can stop AI-generated art. But we need to be prepared and ready for the changes it will soon bring. Because I bet you've already read an article/post/review and seen an image created by an AI and not even known it.

We definitely live in interesting times.

Writing Dry Spells

Some useful techniques to deal with those times when the words just don't come

SOMETIMES YOU MAY REACH A POINT IN YOUR CREATIVE path where the ideas just don't come, where you stare at a blank page, waiting for the words, the inspiration, and there's just…a void.

Other times you might be brimming with ideas, but when it comes time to do the work, you just aren't motivated, or you feel that others will never want to read it, or you say to yourself, *The Earth is going to hell, so what's the point?*

Some call this phase "writer's block," but I prefer to call it a "writer's pause."

You cannot expect to be productive all the time. Marathoners are told to wait *months* after their last marathon to run long-distance again. Weight lifters do not do legs Monday, Tuesday, *and* Wednesday. They alternate days, so they do not injure themselves. Why should writing be any different?

There will be slow days, slog days, days where all you do is put in a comma in the morning and take it out in the afternoon. I used to beat myself up when I reached these pauses. I thought I didn't have what it takes to be a writer. I felt chewed up, dried out, and I despaired.

This was unhealthy, not just for the negative self-talk, but because it's a distortion of the truth. Like physical muscles, the brain needs rest too. Sometimes you may find that the brimming energy you had just last week seems to be gone now. Where did it go? Who knows, but the answer isn't self-criticism (which I've done), or self-medicating (which I've done more of). Both of those will lead to toxic outcomes and diminishing returns. The answer is acceptance.

You have to accept that you won't always be productive, that the tides of creativity ebb and flow, that the verve you have today may not be there tomorrow. And when the inspiration ebbs, here are some things I suggest doing:

1. Most importantly: *accept yourself*. Be kind to yourself. You are human, not a machine, and you cannot always be churning out 2,000 inspired words per day, no matter what that best-selling author of door-stoppers tells you.

2. Rest. Sleep. Reduce your caffeine. Avoid alcohol and drugs. Give your body a break from stress.

3. Exercise. (Once you have enough rest). Go for a walk or go to the gym. Get outside and away from that keyboard.

4. Eat healthy. This goes with the rest and exercise, but if you're constantly snacking on junk food and soda, this will certainly have an effect on your mood.

5. Get out of your own headspace. Sometimes our ego is our own worst enemy. Walk in nature, or go see a movie, or read an immersive book. When we stop thinking about ourselves for a while, a lot of those troubling thoughts vanish like smoke.

6. Make plans with a friend you haven't seen in a while. Talking to them might rekindle old feelings and inspire new ideas.

7. Keep an "inspiration pile." I use this more for my 3D art than my fiction, but I keep a folder on my computer with images that inspire me, and when I feel unmotivated, I look at those images and often get new ideas. What works of art do you find yourself returning to again and again? Keep them close at hand and refer to them when your motivation is low.

8. Step away from the work. Sometimes we get too close to our creations, or we have too much emotional energy invested in a work, and that energy prevents us from

completing it. Step away for a while and work on something else. When you come back to it, it will usually feel fresh.

9.   Travel. If you can, go someplace you have never been. Just being in a new place, with new people can cause the creative fires to rekindle in our brains. I've gotten dozens of story ideas from places I've visited.

10. Keep a journal. Write a daily log of your feelings. A lot of times our anxieties are subconscious, and only by writing them down can we see what's really on our minds. And sometimes, writing down what's troubling us can offer a new perspective and alleviate some of those anxieties.

11. If all else fails, talk to someone. There's no shame in that. We are social creatures, and writing is an isolating pursuit. If you have the privilege of therapy, I highly recommend it.

The absolute *worst* thing you can do when motivation is low is beat yourself up for it. Accept that it's a natural part of the creative cycle, and before long, usually sooner than you think, the ideas will begin to flow again, the motivation will return, and you'll be back before the keyboard churning out words by the hundreds.

In a world with AI, why should anyone keep writing?

Why should you labor to write a story when an AI can create one in seconds?

CHATGPT. OPENAI. STABLEDIFFUSION.

If you haven't heard these words, you will soon. All of the above are AI-generation tools. You give them a prompt of a few words and they spit out software programs, college essays, complex works of art, and more. Beginning in early 2023, the science fiction magazine *Clarkesworld* was inundated with AI-generated submissions after an "influencer" suggested people could make a quick buck selling to the market (hint: they were wrong.)

Around the same time, I turned in a 136,000 word novel to my agent. It took me about two years to write. Now, with a tool like ChatGPT, with a small prompt it can spit out a novel *in seconds*. AI-generated novels are, at least so far, not any good, But there's no reason to think that someday soon someone won't build an AI that can spit out a work that's publishable. If you doubt me, just have a look at some of the art the StableDiffusion folks are generating. You don't have to go to art school or put in 10,000 hours of learning anymore to create a novel or an impressive painting. Now you can just type in a few words and *voila*.

So, why struggle to make art when an AI can do it in seconds? Well, there are lots of reasons to keep making art. I'll list a few here:

FOR THE SHEER JOY OF IT

Remember when you were a kid and all you needed was a pencil and a piece of paper and you could entertain yourself for hours by drawing dragons and castles and spaceships and aliens? Remember how fun that was? Sure, art can be difficult to make sometimes, but it can also be the most rewarding thing a person ever does. There's a deep and abiding satisfaction that comes with *making something yourself* that can't be attained by having someone else do it. Making art is fun.

Do it for yourself

For me, the act of creation is one of the most satisfying things. Recently I've been away from writing for a few weeks because of work, and I feel a difference in my mood. I'm grumpy (or *more* grumpy, as my wife might say). I felt off. But after a day of working on a story or a novel, I always feel lighter, less burdened. Eventually, I want folks to read my fiction, but when I'm immersed in the work, miles deep in some fictional world, I have a sense of flow and happiness that I get in few other places.

Do it for others

At some point, artists usually want someone else to read or see their work. It's *much* more satisfying to have others appreciate something *you labored over* than something that was created for you with minimal effort. They are admiring work *you* created. Not the work someone else did. You're creating something that others might appreciate, and in so doing you're sharing a part of yourself with them.

I still remember the feeling of selling my first story and realizing others would read and (hopefully) enjoy the story I created. There's nothing like it, that sense of sharing. Other than telepathy and certain forms of love, few things can transmit feelings as powerfully as art. Would you rather communicate someone else's message, or your own? How much of yourself do you want to give?

Art is sharing. Art is giving.

Do it for empathy building

Computers don't feel (not yet, at least). They're not independent agents moving through the world, accumulating experiences. But you are. There's something deeply unique about being human. No one has had your experiences exactly as you have. No one has felt your feelings like you. And no one can convey those feelings and experiences like you either. Art has the power of being able to convey thought and emotion like nothing else. Studies have shown that reading fiction builds empathy because it puts readers in the mind of another, often a person far different from themselves. In an increasingly polarized world, doesn't it make sense to try and build bridges of understanding to increase empathy? An AI isn't going to convey the subjective experience of being you, living your life, experiencing your feelings. And though you may not be writing about yourself explicitly, a piece of ourselves always ends up in our work whether we realize it or not.

Nowadays there's too much focus on STEM — Science, Technology, Engineering, and Math. Seldom do we hear mention of the Arts. This is a tragedy of galactic proportions. The acronym should be STEAM, to include the Arts (& Humanities), because even though we have fabulous tech to play with, it means nothing unless we learn use it in a way that benefits humanity as a whole. Arts & Humanities teach us what it means to be human, what it is to be someone else, what it is to live in this painful world. Art teaches people what it means to feel and understand suffering. Without it, we're just creatures moving through space.

We need Art like we need air.

Do it for the challenge

Why learn to play the guitar if you'll never be as good as Jimi Hendrix? Why write songs if you can just go on YouTube and listen to the greatest songs ever written? You do it for the challenge of it. You do it for the satisfaction of learning a new skill. You do it because it's fun. And because you have no idea what you might create. You might actually become a great guitarist. You might actually write songs for the ages. The same is true with any art. You never know how history is going to remember your work, and for all you know you might create something timeless. And even if you don't, even if you never write a hit song or a best-selling novel, there's a joy and satisfaction in knowing that you challenged yourself, worked hard, and created something, no matter how small.

All art is worth something.

DO IT BECAUSE LANGUAGE IS A SKILL

When you use a tool like ChatGPT to write a term paper or a story, you're not learning the intricacies of language. You're not learning how to communicate with words. But when you labor over every word, sentence, paragraph, chapter, and overarching plot, you begin to see how language can be used as a tool. You learn effective communication techniques. And you learn how to read. This isn't just a benefit to you, but to those around you. And a world where people don't communicate effectively or clearly is a poor world, a world with misunderstandings, conflict, and even war. The more effectively you communicate, the better your overall experience will be. And you'll never learn those skills if an AI writes stuff for you.

CREATIVITY IS OUR HUMAN BIRTHRIGHT

Yes, humans aren't the only animals that make and use tools. But we're the only species that makes art. From cave paintings to the Taj Mahal, humans have been making art for *tens of thousands of years*. Give a kid a crayon and what does she do? She *draws*. We make sandcastles and cities. Drum circles and symphony orchestras. The force that compels a kid to scrawl graffiti in an alleyway is the same force that compelled our hominid ancestors to scrawl pictures of the day's hunt on cave walls. We need to express what's internal to us. We need to share our powerful and sometimes overwhelming feelings. We feel compelled to leave our mark on the world, and art is often how we do it.

AI is using other people's work to generate something "new." But there's no individual agency there, no single, unitary entity that said, *This is what I want to bring into the world* and then made it happen. Creativity is who we are. Humanity as a species wouldn't exist without art. And so by abdicating your creative power to a machine, you're giving up a part of what makes you uniquely human.

We make art because art is us. We make art because we must.

Emotional Honesty

Hiding from dark truths can sometimes be detrimental to good art

I WATCHED A SHOW RECENTLY ON NETFLIX. I WON'T NAME the show, because I don't want to spoil it for those who haven't seen it. In the show, someone gets cancer and, though the characters do everything to keep her alive, she ends up dying, leaving behind her grieving friends and family.

But her death was too perfect.

What I mean is, while the show had some poignant moments, I found it emotionally dishonest. They presented her death as a mere "slipping away," sort of like falling asleep, or drifting off into a nap while no one was looking. The woman got to say her goodbyes to all her loved ones, and all her emotional loose ends were neatly tied up when each family member and friend got to say their final goodbyes.

Life is seldom like this. Very often, we don't say all that needs to be said to our family and loved ones before they die. We don't get closure. We don't arrive home in time or we miss our window, or death comes quick and unexpected, and far too soon.

Also, death is seldom "like a finger plucking a hair from a glass of milk" as the Hasids like to say. It's often painful, brutal, and excruciating not just to the dying, but to those who love them.

I'm not trying to depress you, but I want to point out what I felt was emotional dishonesty in a work of fiction. For the sake of providing the viewer emotional comfort, they sacrificed verisimilitude and, in my opinion, turned the show from something that could have been great into something that was merely good.

Some people read fiction to escape reality — and that's okay. Reality can be brutal enough without reading fictional stories about it. And, of course, there are some types of fiction intended to give us the warm and fuzzies, like curling up on a rainy day with a glass of tea, a blanket, and a good book, like the so-called "cozy" mysteries.

But the unfortunate truth is that real life is hard. It's unpredictable. It's brutal. It steals away those we love when we least expect it. And I think if we really want to be comforting, if we really want to write about the human condition, we shouldn't shy away from these painful experiences, but *challenge them head on.*

I'm not saying all writers or artists should do this. Some may not want to go this route. Some may find it too painful or emotionally treacherous.

But for me, I think the best works of art are those that don't shy away from truth, no matter how ugly. Because it's only by reflecting our own humanity back to us that we can understand who and what we are.

And it's what we do with that pain, what we sublimate that pain into, that, in my opinion, makes a work of art great.

Don't Limit Yourself to Just One Medium

Explore your many creative sides

MOST CREATIVE PEOPLE[4] I KNOW HAVE MORE THAN ONE creative hobby. One friend loves to write, but also loves to draw. Another loves writing short stories but also writes music.

One of my own non-writing creative hobbies is making visual art. I drew all throughout my childhood, usually diddling on notebooks and desks. I sketched in college in fits and spurts. Later, I experimented with acrylic painting. It took me a while, but I finally found my home in 3D art.

I started about four years ago, and I was pretty bad at it. But over time, I got better[5].

It's far easier to see an artist's progression in visual art. It's much harder to see their progression in fiction. Not just because prose takes longer to read than looking at a picture, but because the changes can be more subtle. Punchier nouns, stronger verbs, clearer visual descriptions, better dialog, and many other non-quantifiable things. All may be morphing and changing as a writer matures.

I sometimes find that progression in my own visual art skills translates into progression in my writing skills. There's something about translating an image or vision in my head into something tangible that is similar in visual art and fiction. I start with a vision, but as I put words on a page or objects into a scene I have to make minor adjustments to account for

---

4   For the record, I think all people are creative, but I'm specifically referring to those who are artists of one form or another.

5   You can see all of my art here: https://www.matthewkressel.net/category/art/

how my vision differs from reality. Often times, this means I'm be making dozens, if not hundreds of minor adjustments to refine the work. My vision is still compelling me — I almost never compromise it — but the practical considerations of working in a specific medium force me to make choices that alter the work, usually for the better.

The best way to describe it is how a human being is constantly making small, almost invisible adjustments to their musculature in order to walk without falling. You are balancing your body's strength against the pull of gravity. This give and take, when it's perfectly balanced, can result in a "flow" state akin to walking without thinking.

Certainly, visual art and writing are very different skills, but I find the creative expression in one often informs the other. And, lately, when I make 3d art or when I write stories, I find myself in a similar, if not identical mental state, totally focused on refining my work to fit my vision.

Are you a musician? Singer? Painter? Poet? Do you have a garden? Do you like to draw? Sculpt? Make collages? How does one art form inspire and inform the other?

For me, it's like walking different paths in the same immense field. Exploring each gives me a greater sense of my own infinite creative landscape. If you find yourself stuck or blocked in one medium, try switching to another. It may open up new creative pathways for you.

This is How Your (Fictional) World Ends?

Do you need to know how your story ends before you begin?

AT THIS BEGINNING OF THE NEW YEAR, I THOUGHT IT appropriate to talk about endings. Specifically, the endings of stories.

In the previous chapter, "Pantsing vs. Plotting," I discussed the difference between pantsing vs. plotting (or gardeners vs. weeders), that is, those who write without needing to know the ending, and those who outline every detail before they begin.

Here, I want to talk about the *Pantsing* side of things and some techniques I use to propel me along a story without knowing exactly where things are going.

First off, I feel that some authors get stuck needing to know every detail of their story before they begin. "I have this idea," Jane Author says to me, "but I'm not sure where it's going. All I know is that it begins with *Cool Thing #1* and *Cool Thing #2*. After that, I'm stuck."

And because they don't know where the story might lead, they never write it. Which is a shame, because I always think *Cool Things Nos. 1 & 2* are pretty good ideas for a story.

So here's the thing: *You don't need to know where a story is going in order to start writing it.*

YOU DON'T NEED TO KNOW WHERE A STORY IS GOING IN ORDER TO START WRITING IT

I put that in bold because it's an important point. I don't even think you need to know what your story is about. This isn't to say you don't need an idea. I like to think of a story

73

as a tree grown from a seed. You start with a small packet of information: a setting, a character, a challenge — and you give it some water and soil and it grows (often slowly at first) into this huge living thing. It takes on a life of its own.

The next thing I do is practice "active imagination." As a writer, you need to work your imagination every day. It's a muscle, and like any other, it can atrophy if you don't work it out. You imagine yourself as your character in your setting. What would your character see? Feel? Smell? Hear? Taste? Try to imagine every sense. You don't need to necessarily list every sense on the page, but immersing yourself in your character's experience will often tell you exactly what comes next.

As with stories, all writers are different, but I try to ground the reader in character and setting as quickly as possible. Readers like characters. And readers especially like characters that are *doing and feeling things.*

A lot of stories are rejected out of hand because the author did a poor job of grounding the reader in character and setting. If I'm two pages into your story and I still don't know who the main character is, where they are, and what they want, well, for me that's not such an interesting story, and I'm probably going to put it down. Of course, there are exceptions. Sometimes it's fun to uncover the mystery of what's going on. But character and place are almost always important.

Next, I give my characters a challenge, something to stir them to action. This can be as epic as saving the world from a great encroaching evil, or as personal as learning about the death of a loved one.

Action doesn't necessarily mean laser battles and derring-do. It might mean your protagonist has to face an *emotional* challenge. Some of my favorite stories have almost no external action at all. The main challenge is internal, emotional, personal.

A good technique is to force your characters to make a choice. Not something mundane, like to put milk or cream in their coffee. But something with *high personal stakes.* Do they take their dream job across the country, or do they turn down the job to stay home with an ailing parent? Do they take up arms and go to war to save their country, even though they might die? Do they give into the lust of an extramarital affair, even though it might ruin their loving marriage?

Usually, by starting with these two things — character and choice — is enough to propel your story into motion. This is the water and soil that will help your story grow.

The next thing I do is encourage flow. By this I mean, I try to get myself into a flow state. Lots of people will tell you all sorts of mystical crap about flow states. It's really just focused concentration.

You want to tread water in the boundary layer between your conscious, active imagination, and your subconscious, or dream state. You want to constantly be imagining, *What comes next?* If you do this often enough, you will find that stuff will just appear in your head. This is your subconscious working for you. It's doing the hard work of collating and organizing your life experience so you don't have to.

If you listen to your subconscious, it will tell you what comes next. And you *should* listen to it. No, it's not always going to work. Oftentimes, it'll spit out cliches or nonsensical and stupid things. But you can edit those out later. You should actively encourage taking the guardrails off your imagination. Let ideas come into your head and use them, no matter how absurd. You'll find gold there, I promise.

The other thing I do is work to keep the reader in the so-called "fictive dream," as John Gardner called it. This is the familiar feeling of being lost in a story. We've all experienced getting lost in a book, show, or movie. We can do this through several methods:

1.   We keep the story moving forward. This is sometimes known as "narrative tension." Your protagonist wants something, but is continually frustrated. Nevertheless, they are slowly getting closer to their goal. Or the reader senses that the current events will soon come to a head, and the protagonist will have to make a difficult choice. Think of narrative tension like a roller coaster ride. Once you let the cars go at the top of the initial ascent, the rest is all gravity. Your story couldn't stop if it wanted to, because there are unresolved tensions. The reader keeps reading because she wants to know what happens next, and important stuff keeps happening.

2.   We immerse the reader in sense details. We describe colors, smells, tastes, feelings. Don't inundate, but sprinkle with spice. Don't overwhelm the reader with too many details. Give space to let the reader create the story in their mind. But give enough touchstones to let them grab onto your narrative. *Remember: the reader is the author of the story as much as you.*

3.   We keep the sentences smooth and flowing. This is perhaps the hardest of all three techniques. It's the one that's taken me longest to learn. Jeff Ford once said to me something that Lucius Shepard told him: "If you can make shit flow, you can get away with anything." What he means is that if your sentences flow into each other, if they propel the story smoothly forward, the reader will forgive gaps in logic or details. Words have meter and rhythm. One technique I've used to improve my sentence flow is to read them aloud. Awkward sentences and stilted prose become immediately apparent when you read things aloud to yourself. I read all my stories aloud, and it's improved my writing immensely.

Okay, so now we have a good story setup, and our words are flowing. What next? How do we know where to go next?

So I lied a little. When I said you don't need to know where your story ends before you begin, that's true. *But somewhere in this process you do need to find an ending.*

Usually, this should be some kind of resolution of the challenges presented in your beginning. This doesn't mean that everything is solved, or is happily ever after. But something needs to change. Oftentimes, this is your character herself, and their relationship to the world. The questions you asked in the beginning should be answered. The tension should be (mostly) resolved. Otherwise, the reader will feel cheated, or that your story is incomplete. You don't have to answer *everything* — getting your readers to wonder a bit is always good — but most questions should be answered.

Your ending should be emotionally satisfying. This doesn't necessarily mean *happy*, but complete. A good metaphor is music. Great songs don't always end on a happy notes. They could just as easily end on sad ones. But great songs end on an emotionally satisfying tone, not halfway through a chord progression or arpeggio. Use your own emotional judgment to sense where that place is. The worst thing you can do is leave your readers frustrated.

Finally, be wary of the never-ending story. Brandon Sanderson and Alan Moore can write 500,000 word doorstoppers and they'll get published, but the ugly truth is that there are too many distractions today, too many things that can steal our time. I'm not trying to rob you of the experience of writing your twelve-book epic fantasy. But most readers like coming to an ending sooner, rather than later. If you're asking more questions than you are answering, adding more threads than Egyptian silk sheets, it might be time to consider narrowing your focus. A good technique that I like to use is to focus on one specific moment or event, and build my story around that.

Okay, standard disclaimer: these are techniques that I've used but may not necessarily work for you. And they may represent a type of storytelling that may be different from what you're trying to accomplish. The one rule of writing is there are no rules. If my ideas resonate, use them. If not, feel free to ignore them.

I only hope that these suggestions might help you start that story you've been dreading to write because you don't yet know the ending!

Dealing with Rejection

Rejection is a part of the writing life, and the sooner we "get used to it", the better

REJECTIONS HAPPEN.

If you're writing fiction with the intention of being published, at some point you'll want to submit your work to a publisher. And unless you're super lucky, super talented, or both, chances are — being that there are few slots for publication, and editors' time to review your story is already slim (as I've detailed in the previous chapter "The Dreaded First Page") — you will be rejected[6]. That is, the publisher will opt not to publish your work.

But wait! you protest in fury. *I've spent 10,000 hours researching the mating habits of Scandinavian tree lice! I wrote this novel in between caring for a newborn child and holding down six jobs! I poured my heart and soul into this work! How dare you reject me!*

The short of it is, unless you're a steel cage (and I am not), rejections sting. They smart. You work hard on a thing, and all you get back is a one line response: "Thank you, but we are not interested at this time."

This pain is normal. It's frustrating. And it can be heartbreaking, depending on how much emotion you invest in the work. For me, it's usually a lot.

GIVE YOURSELF ROOM TO FEEL, BUT DON'T LET IT STOP YOU

Here's the thing: it's ok to be sad, or frustrated, or upset. This is normal. A few writers told me they don't get bothered by rejections. I don't believe them. I've known a few other writers who were so emotionally invested in their work that they couldn't bear to receive a rejection, and so they asked another person to submit on their behalf.

Whatever you feel is fine. Let yourself feel it. Every editor is just a person in the end, and every person has their tastes and desires. (Just think of how musical tastes vary among your friends.) Your work may not have aligned with what the editor is looking for. It doesn't mean your work isn't good. It just means it isn't for *them*.

Do not respond!

But whatever you do, *Do not respond!* This is super important, so I'll say it again: *do not respond to rejections*. Not only is this considered unprofessional, many editors will get angry with you, and they may block or restrict you from submitting to their publication again.

Sure, that one sentence in their rejection email was real snarky. And they totally didn't appreciate your unbridled genius prose on page 3. But responding to a rejection letter will only get you into trouble. Go vent to your significant other or your cat. I promise you, it will save your career.

Even great writers get rejections

Stephen King in *On Writing* spoke about the spike he hung above his desk. Every time he got a rejection letter (submissions were by postal mail in those days) he hung it on the spike. At one point he had accumulated so many rejections the spike fell off the wall.

James Tiptree, Jr (a.k.a. Alice B. Sheldon) and Ursula K. LeGuin wrote each other letters complaining of rejections. And I've seen veteran editor Ellen Datlow reject stories from veteran authors at the top of their field. It doesn't matter who you are. Rejections are part of the game.

You can try hard and fail — that's just life

As Captain Picard famously said in *Star Trek The Next*

Generation, "It is possible to commit no mistakes and still lose. That is not a weakness. That is life."

It's tempting to take rejections personally, to think the rejection is a comment on your worthiness as a human. But this is not true. It's merely a comment on that particular person feeling your work isn't a good fit for their publication. The fact that they do not take the work is not a reflection on your self-worth. Do not mistake the two.

GET BACK ON THE SADDLE IMMEDIATELY

It's tempting to wallow in self-pity when you get a rejection. You might have a crisis of confidence: *Am I good enough? Do I need to rewrite my story? Should I stop this writing thing altogether?*

My advice: take that story or novel and *immediately send it out to another publisher.* Do not wait. Do not pause. I've seen far to many good writers stop writing because a few rejections spoiled their confidence. Putting your work out there immediately is the best way I've found to lessen the sting of a rejection. If one editor doesn't like your work, maybe another will.

Rejections are a part of the writing life, and having good techniques to handle them will help you along the way. Just remember that it's okay to feel. No one is impervious. But if you really want to build a writing career[6], it's good to have some helpful tools.

---

6   I'm speaking obviously of traditional publishing here. Indy (or self-) publishing doesn't have to deal with rejections in the same way.

Conclusions

My grateful thanks and where you can read more of my work

WELL, THERE YOU HAVE IT! I HOPE YOU FOUND THE ADVICE in this book helpful and practical. I learned a lot from a lot of great people along the way, and my hope is that I passed on some good advice to you.

If you want to read more of my work, You can find a list of all of my novels and short fiction on my website, matthewkressel.net. I do hope you'll check it out!

Each of these chapters was originally posted on my newsletter, *The Outer Deep* (outerdeep.substack.com) and it's totally free to subscribe. You'll find all these chapters (and hopefully some new ones!) archived there.

You can also find a list of all my social media accounts here, if you wish to follow me online:

https://www.matthewkressel.net/contact/

It has been a lot of fun writing this book, and I sincerely thank you for reading it.

Happy writing!

Best,
Matthew Kressel
matthewkressel.net

MATTHEW KRESSEL IS A WRITER AND A SOFTWARE developer. He is a three-time Nebula Award Finalist, a World Fantasy Award Finalist, and a Eugie Award Finalist. *NPR Books* called his first novel *King of Shards*, "Majestic, resonant reality-twisting madness." His many works of short fiction have appeared in such publications as *Lightspeed, Clarkesworld, Analog, Tor.com, Nightmare, Beneath Ceaseless Skies*, and multiple *Year's Best* anthologies, as well as many other anthologies and magazines. His work has been translated into French, Spanish, Russian, Chinese, Czech, Romanian, Polish, Farsi, and Japanese. As a software developer, he created the Moksha submissions system (moksha.io), in use by many of the largest fiction publishers today. And he is the co-host of Fantastic Fiction at KGB reading series in New York beside Ellen Datlow.

READ MORE AT WWW.MATTHEWKRESSEL.NET

www.ingramcontent.com/pod-product-compliance
Lightning Source LLC
Chambersburg PA
CBHW071626040426
42452CB00009B/1511